The Collection
2022

compiled by John Field

EXPRESS NEWSPAPERS

hamlyn

First published in Great Britain in 2021 by Hamlyn,
a division of Octopus Publishing Group Ltd, Carmelite House,
50 Victoria Embankment, London EC4Y 0DZ
www.octopusbooks.co.uk

An Hachette UK Company
www.hachette.co.uk

Cartoons.
British Cartoon Archive

Cartoons supplied by British Cartoon Archive
Cartoons compiled by John Field

ISBN 978 0 60063 658 8

A CIP catalogue record for this book is available from the British Library.

Printed and bound in China

10 9 8 7 6 5 4 3 2 1

Contents

The Kitchen,
19 December 1967

The Giles Family Home

Through Giles's cartoon family, the illustrator portrayed British domestic life during the second half of the 20th century, but with exaggerated attitudes and views emphasised by the idiosyncrasies and foibles of some of its members. Over the almost half century of their existence, members of the family never aged physically, but we saw significant changes in their circumstances as the years went by – including cars, caravans, foreign holidays, yachts, bigger houses and larger gardens.

In fact, the family home itself became both a reflection of Britons' changing circumstances as well as a stage set for the ups and downs of everyday life. As with all his work, Giles was meticulous in showing details within the family home and often, as time passes, we can see changes in the fashions of clothes, furniture, upholstery and the like. This year's collection therefore showcases the family against the backdrop of its natural habitat, and traces Grandma, Mother, Father and the clan going about their full, usually chaotic lives, room by room.

The Hall
With such a large family, 12 members spread over four generations, there is inevitably a great deal of "comings and goings" through the hallway. We see a wide range of visitors, both welcome and unwelcome, entering and departing. Sometimes a cartoon uses the hall as the setting for a serious discussion regarding important family business and, at other times, it is the scene of a confrontation between various family members over issues going on in the wider world. The fact that, in some cartoons, the telephone is located in the hall also causes a medley of family members to congregate there on occasion.

The Lounge
The lounge is one of three rooms in the house where we usually see all, or most, of the family assembled together. However, it is rarely shown as a comfortable family setting with the members happily at ease with each other (where is?). Often there is tension, and even heated debate, over some family drama or a major event in the life of the nation. Sometimes personal grievances or political differences are aired. At other times the discord centres around the misdemeanours of one of the children or Grandma, the outspoken matriarch of the family. The lounge is also the scene of great family occasions, such as Christmas parties or national celebrations, but rarely are these depicted as scenes of peace and familial calm.

The Dining Room,
8 September 1966

The Kitchen

The kitchen is another location where the whole family gathers, allowing Giles again to situate his chaos right in the heart of the home. He particularly enjoyed displaying the family's disorder at Christmas time, when we often see Mother harried and preparing the festive feast, while various other family members are interrupting, interfering or oblivious to her endeavours. The kitchen cartoons are particular favourites as they allow Giles to display his flair for disarray and the unfortunate circumstances that often cause Mother's best-laid-plans to spiral out of control.

The Dining Room

This is the third location in the house where major family gatherings occur. It is where we most often see the whole family, or a substantial part of it, together, its members gathered at the table for a relatively long period of time. They are in close proximity and this provides an excellent occasion for grievances, debates and dramas to be aired. It is not surprising, given her character, that Grandma is often seen to be in the thick of many of the disagreements although she is rarely seated at the table. The other family members' individual personalities are also fully expressed in this setting: Mother personifying her low-key control of the household; Father attempting to assert authority; daughter-in-law Vera, with her baby George Jr., looking worried; George, her husband, either deep in thought or reading a book; Young Ernie and the twins frequently up to no good; Bridget, the youngest daughter, often (but not always) trying to be helpful; and Ann and Carol, the older daughters with other things on their minds.

The Stairs and Landing

This is, by its very nature, another setting for movement within the house, allowing usually brief, but often telling, interactions to be played out on the move between various family members. It is the scene of passing conversations and overheard comments as the relatives mention complaints, secrets, plans and grievances, usually sowing the seeds for further misunderstandings.

The Bedroom

Mother and Father's bedroom is often used as the setting for various family events, such as Mothers' Day. From time to time, Grandma's bedroom and those of the children also appear. These cartoons show, again, a scene of confusion

*The Bathroom,
14 March 1965*

and family disorientation and their humour often relies upon a situation where the preparations for an event have gone badly wrong (usually some child has prepared a present that backfires, Father has forgotten the date or Grandma, as expected, is unhappy with her gift).

The Bathroom
The setting for only a small number of family cartoons, the bathroom nonetheless crops up occasionally when Giles displays his skill in emphasising a cacophony of small details. He seems to delight in the hostilities that occur when various family members are forced to share a small space, such as Father's unmitigated irritation at the presence of younger family members and their variety of bath-time accoutrements filling up his house.

The Garden
Even outside in the garden the family's activities and its often exuberant behaviour usually produces a high level of discord and confusion. The open space allows Giles to be more adventurous with the family, so that its activities are more free-ranging and less controlled, covering gardening, sport and various construction works, including tree houses.

In the garden, the children often manage to get up to all sorts of mischief out of the adults' sight, while the attempts of the older members of the family to relax are usually rudely disturbed by some form of activity being pursued by the younger members.

The Giles family's natural habitat
What's abundantly clear is that Giles greatly enjoyed creating and illustrating this unruly family and allowing its various idiosyncrasies to grow and flourish. He deliberately created a family with many faults and contradictions and, although over the years the family turned up in a range of different locations, it is obvious that in their natural habitat they can most fully display their real characters. And Giles can cast a bright light upon the complex relationships within.

I hope that readers enjoy this year's collection showing the Giles family members living their complex lives within the setting of the family home. It is their chaotic lifestyle that has made the family so entertaining and memorable, and what has given me a great deal of pleasure in compiling this collection.

John Field

The Hall

I have a feeling that Father's sense of wellbeing and confidence that all is well with the world is about to be shattered.

"His Royal Highness – King of the Office Parties – home bang on time as usual to help with the decorations."

Sunday Express, 23 December 1956

The 1958 FIFA World Cup, played in Sweden, ran from the 8–29 June and received considerable TV coverage in Britain. The weather during that month was recorded as being "very wet, dull and rather cool", hence the menfolk's appearance. The Wimbledon Championships started the day before this cartoon appeared and the note from the women of the family makes it clear that it is now their turn.

"In view of the recent soaking we have had of World Series Football on TV and radio, there will be no complaints from certain members of the family during the next two weeks of Wimbledon tennis."

Daily Express, 24 June 1958

Father, having obviously sampled a few festive drinks, is taking the period of goodwill a bit too far.

"Mum! Dad's just given the carol singers a cheque for five million pounds."

Sunday Express, 23 December 1962

Giles, an avid sailor with his own large yacht, frequently referred to the annual Boat Show at Earls Court in his cartoons. Here, I suspect, Mother is making a point about having to face cleaning up after the festive period without any help, while the rest of the family are already engrossed with the next major event.

"'Afternoon, Your Highness, 'afternoon, Lord Mountbatten, 'afternoon, Mr. Chichester – so nice of you to come along to advise us on our choice of luxury cruiser."

Daily Express, 3 January 1967

14   The day before, telephone charges to the United States had been reduced from £3 to £2.10s for the first three minutes. Father does not seem to be convinced that, in the long run, his telephone bills will be cheaper.

"Get in the queue if you want to take advantage of the new reduced telephone charges to the United States."

Daily Express, 2 February 1967

This appeared in the newspaper the day after the Apollo 11 spaceflight was launched. Three days later, Commander Neil Armstrong became the first person to step onto the lunar surface with his famous quote, "That's one small step for man, one giant leap for mankind". The whole flight was the subject of great interest around the world.

"Kindly inform your mother that Earth Man is home and wants his tea."

Daily Express, 17 July 1969

16 Looking at Father's clock, this was just before the kick-off of the much-awaited match at the Estadio Azteca in Mexico City, between Mexico and the Soviet Union. The final score was a 0–0 draw and the winner of the overall tournament, three weeks later, was Brazil. Father's plans are in for a slight setback.

"Now who's going to tell him Uncle Ernie and Auntie Rosie and the children are coming to tea?"

Sunday Express, 31 May 1970

Father is preparing for the UK joining of the European Economic Community, which was in the early stage of negotiations, with the final entry not taking place until January 1973. Mademoiselle Suzie may not live up to his expectations.

"Allee Oops! Mademoiselle Suzie de Pompadour is here to begin your 'Learn-French-at-Home' course."

Sunday Express, 14 November 1971

The average rate of inflation during 1973 was 9.18 per cent and the government was imposing stringent financial constraints to control it. Father's face perfectly illustrates his feelings on the subject.

"The house is on fire and I've broken my leg apprehending a burglar – ask your dad if it's all right for me to dial 999."

Daily Express, 29 March 1973

Father has the habit of giving his daughter's musical boyfriends appropriate names based upon well-known singers and musicians.

"Tell Carol ol' blue eyes is here."

Daily Express, 17 May 1975

Giles is expressing his thoughts on some of the Arts Council's purchases at that time.

"Go and tell Dad Auntie Florrie's pup has just created a little work of art in the hall."

Sunday Express, 17 October 1976

The day before, it was reported in the newspapers that gold prices were "soaring at a record rate in wild trading". As usual, Grandma is overreacting and the family pets, and the twins, are not keen on this possible addition to the household.

"Grandma – is this your ad. in the local paper? 'WANTED, Guard dog for now very valuable gold wedding ring'."

Daily Express, 20 September 1979

Giles's comment on the grape-harvesting season. Presumably there should be a health warning on every bottle of wine produced by this particular viticulturist.

"It's a summons from a burglar who broke in and stole half a bottle of Grandma's home-made wine and has never been the same since."

Sunday Express, 26 September 1982

"He's not to have those till Christmas – back where you found them!"

Sunday Express, 18 December 1988

The Lounge

The British economy was in a very poor state, still suffering from the effects of the War. But Vera, who was obviously a great fan of American singer Frank Sinatra, was more concerned about negative press reports coming from America concerning his alleged Mafia connections at the time.

"Perhaps you realise now, Vera, that if you'd thought more about your country and less about Frank Sinatra we wouldn't be in the mess we are now."

Daily Express, 12 March 1948

Oops, Mother could be in trouble. There are only five children in the Giles family, including grandson George Jr., but I can count six here.

"Never mind – it must have been today's I gave them, to cut up for chains."

Daily Express, 20 December 1949

The natural succession in a young boy's year. The B.R.M. Type 15 was a Formula One racing car at the time while the Manx Grand Prix motorcycle races are held on the Isle of Man's TT Course in early September. The 15th September 1940 was officially named Battle of Britain Day as it was the day when RAF Fighter Command claimed a decisive victory over the German Luftwaffe.

"Come in, Jim – we're finished being B.R.M.s – we're Isle of Man riders until Saturday, when we'll be Battle of Britain pilots."

Daily Express, 13 September 1950

Changeable weather prevailed throughout March, with persistent clouds and rain and some wintry showers. Carol was obviously unprepared for the weather or the motorbike.

"Here comes Sis's young man on a LOVELY NEW MOTOR-BIKE!"

Daily Express, 30 March 1951

28 It was widely anticipated that the Budget Day speech, to be given a few days later by the Chancellor of the Exchequer, Rab Butler, would stress the grave financial situation confronting the country in the postwar years. The pet shop man obviously used this concern to work upon Vera's compassion for living things. At least Vera's son, George Jr., looks pleased.

"The man in the pet shop told Vera that all his little birds would starve after Budget Day unless somebody bought them."

Daily Express, 7 March 1952

Grandma, never slow to point out other people's faults and shortcomings, is here commenting upon the continuous illnesses of her granddaughter-in-law, Vera. The mounting costs of the NHS were being debated in Parliament at the time.

"If it wasn't for people like Vera we wouldn't want a health service."

Daily Express, 29 March 1952

Although Carl and his wife, Joan, never had children, his cartoons often illustrate his pleasure in observing and capturing the typical child's attitude towards adult aspirations. Wartime sweets and chocolate rationing started in July 1942 and ended two days before this cartoon's appearance.

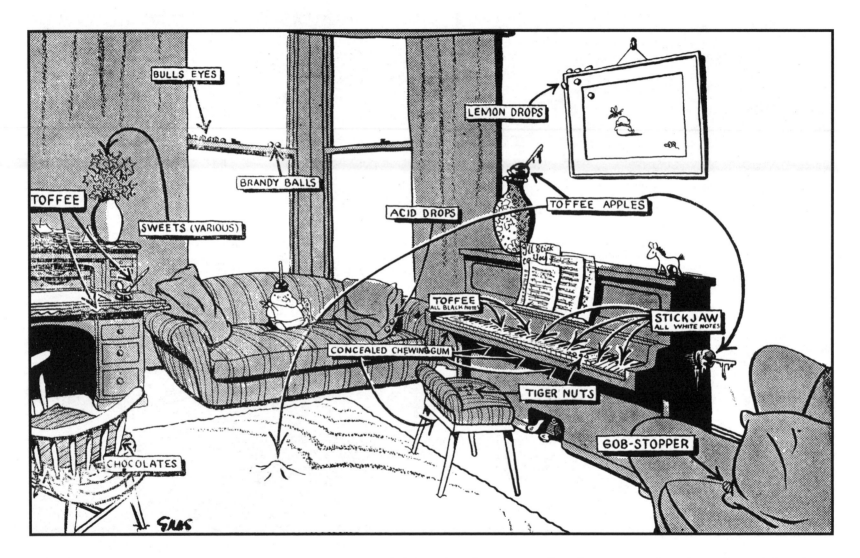

"IN THE GILES FAMILY there is a theory among the children that the more toffee they get on the piano the quicker they get their music lessons over – you press one note and they all go down together. I offer this simple sweets-are-now-off-the-ration guide to parents who, during the more or less sweet-free years, may have forgotten the trouble spots."

Daily Express, 7 February 1953

We do not know which horse Grandma put her money on but American-bred Never Say Die won the Derby this year. His jockey, Lester Piggott, won his first of a record-breaking nine Derby victories.

"I for one ain't going to be around if Johnny Longden upsets your grandma's system."

Daily Express, 1 June 1954

After her coronation in 1953, the Queen undertook a number of visits to parts of the Commonwealth never before visited by her predecessors. Two days before this cartoon appeared, she arrived in Nigeria for an 18-day visit.

"RIGHT! That'll be enough good-will messages to Nigeria for to-day."

Daily Express, 31 January 1956

This was a week before Mayflower II sailed from Plymouth, recreating the original 1620 voyage across the Atlantic to the New World.

33

"Why's Dad trying to book a single reservation on the Mayflower?"

Sunday Express, 14 April 1957

Sixteen nuclear bomb tests were conducted during 1957 by the USSR during the Arms Race between the USA and the Soviet Union.

"The President of the Peace Loving Movement then added that Russia's latest H-bomb, if dropped on the North Pole, was capable of melting all the snow and ice, which would flood London in a matter of minutes. Which wouldn't do that cold of yours any good, Vera."

Daily Express, 4 June 1957

The Arms Race and the Space Race between the USA and the Soviet Union were each at their height. A couple of months earlier, the world's first artificial satellite, Sputnik 1, was launched by the USSR and was about to drop back to Earth. At the same time, the British Government was expressing concern that US bombers, operating from British bases, were carrying hydrogen bombs. Grandma's words probably did not help in reassuring ailing Vera.

"In any case you'll never know what hit you – an American going home lit with an H-bomb or a Sputnik landing back on earth."

Sunday Express, 1 December 1957

On this day, World War II US General, Dwight Eisenhower, met Britain's wartime
Prime Minister, Winston Churchill, in London.

"Well – since they ask – why AREN'T you with Britain's wartime top brass at Ike's party tonight?"

Daily Express, 1 September 1959

"Come away from that window and stop shouting 'Here come some more'."

Sunday Express, 10 January 1960

38

Rawhide was a hugely popular American Western TV programme. On this occasion, its broadcast was conflicting with the opening day of the 1960 Olympic Games being held in Rome. Intriguingly, Giles has not given us a clue as to which programme Grandma is rooting for.

"Next one who switches RAWHIDE on in the middle of my Olympic Games – BED!"

Daily Express, 25 August 1960

Anna Mary Robertson Moses, known by her nickname Grandma Moses, was an American folk artist who began painting in earnest at the age of 77. In the USA, her 100th birthday, the day before this cartoon appeared, was proclaimed "Grandma Moses Day". I wonder what Grandma Giles made of the subject on that great blank canvas?

"That was a bright stroke telling Grandma there is a famous Grandma-artist in America who is 100 years old and didn't take up painting till she was 77."

Daily Express, 6 September 1960

This appeared five days before the 15th Session of the UN General Assembly in New York, at which many world leaders were present.

"With all UNO playing about in New York it's a fine opportunity for Red China to take over the world."

Daily Express, 21 September 1960

The following Saturday's matches were under threat as the 2,000 members of the Professional Footballer's Association were threatening to strike in a wages and contracts dispute. I suspect Ernie will have some system in place to ensure that it is not him who has to break the news.

"In view of the circumstances I think we'll cut cards for who tells Dad the cat got three of his racing pigeons."

Daily Express, 19 January 1961

The day before, it was reported that the Russians had detonated a Tsar Bomb (at 11:32 Moscow Time) over the Mityushikha Bay nuclear testing range, north of the Arctic Circle, at a height of 4,000m above the target.

"That wasn't a fifty-megatoner or an earthquake – that was Grandma's tummy rumbling."

Daily Express, 31 October 1961

Father is again speaking his mind, but the question is, who put the microphone there?

43

"Hold it, folks – listen to a recording made a few minutes ago of someone saying: 'Which do you hate most, his summer holiday films or his damn dog doing tricks?'"

Sunday Express, 24 December 1961

Acker Bilk was a British clarinetist and vocalist. It had recently been reported that theatre musicians planned a strike to protest over pay claims.

"Tell Acker Bilk he's got his first fan mail – from the people next door asking when he's joining the Musicians' strike."

Daily Express, 24 May 1962

The winter of 1963 was one of the coldest in memory. Snow swept across the country on Boxing Day 1962 and stayed on the ground in many areas until late March, causing football matches to be called off. The sheriff has discovered an effective way of keeping the children occupied.

"I told him as there's no football he can stay at home and amuse the children."

Sunday Express, 20 January 1963

The 1963 Derby was to be run the next day and was won by Relko, a French thoroughbred racehorse. It is not recorded if Grandma's hard work paid off. It appears that George Jr. is a little concerned about the security of the piggy bank.

"When Grandma starts studying form watch your piggy-banks, I always say."

Daily Express, 28 May 1963

At Wimbledon this year, a Russian player Alex Metreveli withdrew from the men's singles to avoid playing South Africa's Abe Segal, as part of the Soviet Union's wider protest against apartheid. This is not the first time that Father has shown his antipathy towards tennis.

"I'm all for the Russians refusing to play the South Africans – a few hours less of bonk, bonk, thirteigh forteigh."

Sunday Express, 28 June 1964

48 Obviously, this is considered by a certain member of the family to be a very serious crime. However, it seems a bit extreme to apply this draconian interpretation of the family court, complete with a bewigged judge (who in this case, is also the aggrieved party), a barrister (a sibling of the defendant), and an armed police guard. I am not convinced that poor little George Jr. is going to get a fair trial.

"This Family Court charges you with unlawfully swigging Grandma's stout through a straw."

Daily Express, 26 August 1965

An increase of over 14 per cent in electricity charges had just been introduced, which explains Father's sarcastic reference to Andrés Segovia – a virtuoso Spanish classical guitarist very popular at that time. Note the rural scene on the wall; at this time, Giles was carrying on a vendetta against the Central Electricity Generating Board about a line of gigantic pylons which had been constructed across his farm.

"Purely in the interest of power economy, Segovia – purely in the interest of power economy."

Sunday Express, 3 September 1967

The day before, the BBC launched its new Radio One station to provide all-day pop music, intending to replace the pirate radio stations that had been banned by the Marine Broadcasting Offences Act. It was publicised as the "swinging new radio service". It is not known which words Father used but there is no doubt that they were not complimentary. Only Grandma was not shocked by his choice.

"As a matter of fact that's EXACTLY what I said in front of the children about their new Radio One."

Sunday Express, 1 October 1967

"Instant flu-cure coming up – tell your father wee Jock wants to know if he can come out for a New Year drink."

Sunday Express, 31 December 1967

The Divorce Reform Act 1969 was going through Parliament at this time and various aspects of the causes and effects of matrimonial discord were being discussed.

"It is the easiest thing in the world for a child to detect that you're not really listening to him."... Marriage Guidance Council.

Daily Express, 20 June 1969

This was a period of widespread strikes by school teachers over pay. Grandma's home teaching is displaying her unique approach to preparing children for adult life as she sees it.

"Mum, are you sure Grandma's the right one to be carrying on their lessons while the teachers are on strike?"

Daily Express, 19 February 1970

54   Mother is obviously relishing a nice cup of tea in front of the fire and an early morning trip to the Boat Show is the last thing on her mind. Father is raring to go – a change from the situation 17 years later (see cartoon dated 5 January 1988 in the Bedroom chapter).

"Ahoy there, Mummy – The Press Gang's here to take you to the Boat Show."

Daily Express, 5 January 1971

"Me jealous? No! They practically live in the kitchen since I engaged an au pair girl to help."

56   Olga Korbut was a world-famous Soviet gymnast who competed in the 1972 and 1976 Olympic Games, winning four gold medals and two silver. She captured attention around the world, obviously including the Giles family. The FA Cup final had been held the day before and second-division team Sunderland unexpectedly beat Leeds United – the previous season's winners.

"Thank little Olga for taking their minds off football."

Sunday Express, 6 May 1973

The post-festive season tidy up. The Three-Day Week was introduced by the government in order to conserve electricity after shortages caused by the 1973–74 oil crisis. From 1 January that year, commercial users of electricity were limited to three specified consecutive days' usage each week. Butch is supporting his master's "stand" on this important issue.

"Do you think it would infringe the principles of his three-day week if he joined our seven-day week and let down a few balloons?"

Sunday Express, 6 January 1974

58 Unusually, there were two general elections this year, the second in October. In neither case did any communist candidate succeed in becoming a Member of Parliament. On 1 January, the Communist Party produced a new election manifesto entitled "Challenge business – build a new Britain". It looks as if Ernie had read it and succeeded in persuading the younger children of the family to follow his political thinking.

"You are entitled to your own political beliefs regardless of race, religion or colour, but you will kindly refrain from calling the rest of us 'Brothers'."

Sunday Express, 10 February 1974

Butch is about to be in trouble again, this time with Auntie Ivy, and the twins' toy train is about to get them into trouble with Grandma.

"The Supreme Champion of this house has just eaten one of Auntie Ivy's shoes."

Sunday Express, 9 February 1975

This seems beyond normal police powers but Father appears to be aiding and abetting.

"Giving the police extra powers doesn't entitle their new copper boyfriends to monopolise my electric Highway Patrol!"

Sunday Express, 11 January 1981

Ernie and Bridget have discovered the potential value of phone tapping, much to the discomfort of their father. Grandma's parrot is up to one of its favourite tricks.

"Fleet Street will give a bomb for this tape of what Dad said when Aunt Florrie phoned to say they were all coming to tea."

Sunday Express, 10 May 1981

Three weeks earlier, the ten-week conflict between Argentina and the UK over the Falkland Islands commenced. Father is recalling a phrase from World War II. Grandma's parrot is up to one of his tricks.

"Out come the old '39–'45 war jokes – 'If you want to help our boys you should send those socks to the enemy'."

Sunday Express, 25 April 1982

The first ever national water strike was entering its second week with the industry's workers seeking an increase on their basic wage comparable with those of workers in similar industries such as gas and electricity. One has sympathy with the children's concern.

"We've got to sign an agreement that in the event of a future water shortage no way will they have to share a bath with Grandma."

Sunday Express, 23 January 1983

64 This was during the build-up to the 1983 general election. Yuri Andropov was the sixth paramount leader of the Soviet Union and had been Chairman of the KGB, whereas Screaming Lord Sutch was a serial parliamentary candidate and founder of the Official Monster Raving Loony Party. Of course, Mrs Thatcher was Prime Minister at this time and had earned the nickname the Iron Lady. Vince had a real problem.

"Dad this is Vince – he's torn between Mrs. Thatcher, Andropov and Screaming Lord Sutch."

Sunday Express, 15 May 1983

Many things were going wrong at this time with a number of strikes taking place, the value of the pound plummeting and the football news making Grandma even more sour than normal (particularly with the parrot having stolen her glasses again). The latest information from the policeman about Ernie is unlikely to raise the family's spirits.

"We have a report that your boy is celebrating Trafalgar Day on top of Nelson's column."

Sunday Express, 21 October 1984

66 An outstandingly bad summer: in some parts of Britain, it was the wettest so far during the 20th century, and the coldest for 50 years. Counting up the children, I am not sure whose hands are pulling the tablecloth. And could that be Stinker, the neighbour's son, giving Grandma a trim?

"You must make allowances for them getting bored with non-stop rain and Scrabble."

Sunday Express, 11 August 1985

A policy of Glasnost (openness) between great world powers had started two years earlier. This cartoon appeared in the middle of a five-day summit in Moscow between US President Ronald Reagan and the Soviet Union's Mikhail Gorbachev, which finalized the Intermediate-Range Nuclear Forces Treaty. Giles hated football hooliganism and is inferring that Chelsea, which had a bad reputation at this time, should be kept out of any football tournament in Russia to protect the new period of friendship.

"It's keep Chelsea out of Moscow or bye-bye Glasnost."

Daily Express, 31 May 1988

Just one more skirmish in the ongoing battle between Grandma and her grandchildren. Two days earlier, Prime Minister Margaret Thatcher had confirmed "we are a grandmother", a phrase normally only used by royalty.

"'We are a Grandmother', but I don't think 'we' are amused."

Sunday Express, 5 March 1989

Grandma is not known for compassion and it looks as if one of her grandchildren may have inherited her genes.

69

"Why should I let him win as it's Father's Day? Check mate!"

Sunday Express, 18 June 1989

The Dining Room

Ten days earlier, a US bomber had accidentally jettisoned an unarmed nuclear weapon over Georgia in the USA and questions were asked in Parliament about the possibility of such an accident happening in the UK.

"Honey, will you kindly explain to your Mama that not every top-sergeant at the Base is radioactive."

Daily Express, 22 March 1958

The two defendants look both hostile and guilty. I am not sure they will have a fair trial in this court.

"We've been studying this Express Inquiry into Parenthood and we've decided that you and Grandma will have to leave home."

Daily Express, 3 March 1960

The Derby horse race had been held the day before and, obviously, Grandma's horse St. Paddy was the winner.

Angry Silence. Grandma tipped everybody also-rans but backed the winner herself.

Daily Express, 2 June 1960

This was a time of strong political turmoil in the country. Prime Minister Harold Wilson had introduced a pay freeze two months earlier, much to the anger of Frank Cousins, General Secretary of the Transport and General Workers' Union, who resigned as Minister of Technology.

"Anybody taking the minutes of this top-level conference?"

Daily Express, 8 September 1966

This is the morning of Father's Day and he is lucky, noting the most likely culprit in the family, that there is any left at all.

"Who's been having a go at the bottle of whisky we bought Dad for Father's Day?"

Sunday Express, 20 June 1971

At this time, the miners were picketing power stations and all other sources of fuel supply in the sixth week of a strike over pay. Four days before this cartoon appeared, the Central Electricity Generating Board had announced that many homes and businesses would be without electricity for up to nine hours a day. Ernie's kind gesture was not fully appreciated by many members of the family.

"Dad, I forgot to tell you I asked my friend's people to lunch as they've got a power cut."

Sunday Express, 20 February 1972

The Minister of Agriculture, Fisheries and Food had just reported that the cost of meat had risen by almost 25 per cent during the previous two years. Presumably Ernie felt that this information would be of interest to their visitors.

"Uncle Percy's little piece of beef cost 35p. Aunt Ivy's little piece of beef cost 35p..."

Sunday Express, 4 June 1972

Three days earlier, Mrs Thatcher had won the general election in a landslide victory and started her second term as Prime Minister, emphasising the need for strict financial policies.

"I hope the Prime Minister makes a better job of her carving than your father."

Sunday Express, 12 June 1983

To mark its success in this year's 24 Hours of Le Mans race, the Jaguar car company announced the XJR-S Celebration Le Mans Coupé. As a limited-edition tribute to one of the most iconic wins in British motorsport history, only 100 of these vehicles were produced. Possibly not the best car to meet the Giles family's needs but Father can dream.
The twins are again causing George Jr. some distress.

"If you're planning on a new family car, remember, I shall be casting a vote."

Daily Express, 20 October 1988

The Kitchen

One of the first of many Giles cartoons showing Father happily walking into a minefield at the beginning of the festive period. The cartoon also shows the cartoonist's love of capturing the utter chaos of the family's kitchen at this time of the year.

"I seem to remember a lot of brave talk this morning about not having a drink with the boys and coming home early to help us."

Daily Express, 24 December 1947

The country was still suffering the rationing of some foodstuffs, including meat, and the family has taken to heart the government's request for the country to produce more food. The vet at the door may not be too impressed by the turkey's situation, and is that Grandma in the chair with a revolver?

"Now if only Vera hadn't read about the necessity for this country to produce more food…"

Daily Express, 24 November 1949

One of many Mother's Day upsets in the Giles household, not helped this time by the family cat, Natalie, producing another large litter of kittens.

"I should have thought we could have managed without your contribution to Mother's Day."

Sunday Express, 19 March 1950

Giles himself was not a great fan of Wimbledon fortnight and, over the years, used his cartoons to make this very clear.

"Bonk, bonk, love-fifteen...bonk, bonk, fifteen-all...bonk, bonk, fifteen-thirty...bonk, bonk, thirty-all...bonk, bonk, thirty-forty... bonk, bonk, deuce...radio and TV for two whole glorious weeks."

Daily Express, 21 June 1955

This cartoon may have been inspired by the cartoonist himself having just acquired a new puppy. I am not sure what Grandma's intentions are, but something appears to have happened to that hat of hers.

"Come and say 'Good Morning' to what you called 'The sweetest Christmas present you have had'."

Daily Express, 27 December 1956

This was the day after the Grand National at Aintree. The winning horse was Kilmore, a 28/1 outsider that obviously had not been Father's choice. Note that gambling enthusiast, Grandma, appears to be smiling.

"You're out of his reach – ask him how went the Sport of Kings yesterday."

Daily Express, 27 March 1962

In mid-January 1963, Arctic winds brought much snow and very cold temperatures to Britain in the 'Big Freeze'.
Power cuts became the norm due to extra high demand for electricity.

"It wasn't the power cut – I just switched the light off."

Daily Express, 15 January 1963

This cartoon appeared four days before the Miss World competition, which was won by Carole Crawford of Jamaica.
I am not sure that Grandma would have got through the first stage.

"Good morning, Miss World."

Sunday Express, 3 November 1963

"You can relax now, Vera – they've caught the wolf and denied the escaped puma story."

Daily Express, 16 February 1965

Mother always sees the bright side of things, but Grandma is subdued and making sure that George Jr. does not make a sound.

"I think he's nicer in the mornings since he gave up drinking."

Daily Express, 10 October 1967

"Mum, can our Arms to South Africa debating group use the front room on Christmas Eve?"

Daily Express, 19 December 1967

During the 1960s, the miniskirt had been fashionable but started to fall from favour and the 'maxi' began to take over. Giles infers that high fashion has now caught up with Grandma.

"That puts Grandma bang on target."

Daily Express, 27 January 1970

Most of the family were glued to the TV watching Wimbledon. Obviously Father, never a great lover of tennis, was fending for himself in the kitchen with fairly disastrous results, which is unlikely to reduce his ambivalence about tennis.

"Mum told me to give you a standing ovation for boiling your own egg."

Daily Express, 28 June 1973

The rail strike was part of a period of severe industrial disputes which led to the general election later that month.

"Do I detect a less fervent support of the train drivers' cause now that he can't get to his team's away match because of no trains on Sunday?"

Sunday Express, 3 February 1974

This is not the first time that George Jr. has discovered a small bird in his boiled egg (see cartoon dated 27 March 1962).

"Grandma will be letting off howls of anguish if Mr. Healey finds out she's got a Haig bottle full of sixpences under her bed."

Daily Express, 26 March 1974

Father's situation is far graver than that of George, his son, who only has his wife Vera to appease. Father will have to contend with both his wife and his mother, the formidable and touchy Grandma.

"In the fever and excitement of yesterday's F.A. quarter finals, I hope you all remembered the Mother's Day flowers."

Sunday Express, 9 March 1975

"I've written and told the *Express* the only way they can solve my Christmas present problem is by sending me a cheque."

Daily Express, 4 December 1975

The Third Cod War, between Iceland and the UK, began after Iceland extended its fishing limits to 200 nautical miles from its coast. The British Government did not recognise the large extension to the exclusion zone and problems occurred when British fishermen continued fishing within the disputed area. The dispute lasted from November 1975 until June 1976 and caused a shortage of fish in the UK.

"Grandma, with a grave international crisis over the future of cod you're not supposed to give yours to the cat."

Daily Express, 26 January 1976

The play, *The Romans in Britain*, was first staged at the National Theatre in London five days previously. It explored imperialism and the abuse of power and became the subject of an unsuccessful private prosecution for gross indecency. Obviously Miss Potter gave the abridged version.

"Miss Potter in History taught us all they did was land over here and build good roads."

Daily Express, 21 October 1980

Lord Archer was convicted on two counts of perjury and two of perverting the course of justice after a seven-week trial that saw the politician and bestselling author exposed as a calculating liar who corrupted his friends and employees to secure victory in his libel action against the *Daily Star* newspaper. Maybe Grandma is an admirer of Lord Archer's novels.

"Grandma, can we have breakfast without your verdict on the Archer verdict?"

Sunday Express, 26 July 1987

"We sure got sex-equality in this house – he's switched the washing machine on and lifted the ironing board from the cupboard all on his own."

The House of Commons was debating whether to allow live transmission of its debates. Obviously, Father had had enough of politics without having it on TV as well.

"Right, I've just sold the TV set!"

Daily Express, 9 February 1988

It may be that, at this stage of the celebrations, Mother and the other women in the family agree.

101

"Dad says the Germans have got it right banning Forces Christmas parties in Germany – he says he's for banning Christmas parties everywhere."

Daily Express, 20 December 1988

The Bedroom

The children are anticipating the thrills of the Festival, which was not due to open until more than three weeks after this cartoon appeared. Budget morning is never a good time to approach Father, particularly with any physical activity.

"Perhaps father doesn't feel like playing Festival of Britain switchbacks on Budget morning."

Daily Express, 10 April 1951

Another thing to further darken Father's mood on Budget Day.

103

"And only last night Dad was saying whatever the Budget result things couldn't get much worse."

Daily Express, 11 March 1952

Luckily he did not forget the turkey and maybe that is a bottle of gin for Grandma, which would avoid another source of severe aggravation.

"This delegation wishes to register a strong protest about Father Christmases who come home late and forget to fill our socks."

Sunday Express, 25 December 1955

The first Bob-a-Job week was organised by the UK Scouting movement in 1949 and proved to be a huge success. It became a strong tradition that would last in various guises until the 1990s. With the launch of Community Week in May 2012, the tradition has now been revived. I feel that the family is overdoing it a little in recognising Ernie's new-found importance.

"That Scoutmaster said something when he said Scouts deserve a well-earned rest after their strenuous bob-a-job week."

Sunday Express, 13 April 1958

This was the day after the Budget was broadcast. Alan Tait, a political writer, started his report with the words "Few writers actually enjoy being depressing at the outset of an article but it is my unfortunate duty to draw your attention immediately to the sobering table below." Father's concern about Ernie's investment can be fully understood given the circumstances at that time.

"The man in the pet shop told us to buy tortoises in case they put a tax on tortoises."

Daily Express, 18 April 1961

Not the best start for Father on Mother's Day, particularly with Ernie trying to profit from his mistake.

"Dad – what's it worth if we don't tell Mum you've forgotten Mother's Day?"

Another unpromising start to her Mother's Day – the chimney is on fire, Grandma appears to have had an accident and Father is about to have an unfortunate trip.

"Dad says it's Mother's Day and you're to relax and have breakfast in bed and we'll look after the house..."

Sunday Express, 24 March 1963

Grandma's broad sporting interests have revealed Father's deep concern in pursuing economic measures – even when it comes to Mother's Day.

"This is the same one as you gave me last year – I wrote the 1969 Grand National odds on the bottom."

Sunday Express, 8 March 1970

110 Father is having a Sunday morning lie-in, but it is just after 10 o'clock and the children are obviously keen to share their present with him. One possible concern, however, is whether one of the tadpoles has already turned into a frog, as noticed by the children's friend, Stinker.

"Wake up dear, 'tis Father's Day. Joint presentation – one jar of tadpoles."

Sunday Express, 16 June 1974

Denis Healey was Chancellor of the Exchequer from March 1974 to May 1979 and this cartoon appeared at the time of his 1975 Budget. Father obviously had strong views on the subject and was making life difficult for the family.

"Sign please – 'I do solemnly swear when I come down we will not have Denis Healey for breakfast'."

Sunday Express, 13 April 1975

Mother is using the children to make her thoughts known to Father.

"I suppose your mother financed you for this Father's Day joke."

Sunday Express, 19 June 1977

Easy mistake to make but I suspect Father may say a couple of words to Ernie.

113

"Sorry Mum, I put all the clocks back instead of forward, and Uncle Charlie and all of them have arrived for lunch."

Sunday Express, 19 March 1978

114   Grandma was incensed at the news that the government was proposing to appoint Sir Ian MacGregor for the top job at British Steel and that it would pay up to £1.8m to the US merchant bank Lazard Freres as compensation for losing a senior partner.

"I wouldn't get up yet – Grandma's still sounding off about paying £2 million transfer fees with her money."

Sunday Express, 4 May 1980

This was a week into the month-long 12th FIFA World Cup in Spain. With several matches every day, perhaps even Father would be tired. Hopefully he came round in time for that day's England–Czechoslovakia match, which England won 2–0.

"Awake my love, 'tis Father's Day – for a special treat you've got football all the afternoon on TV."

Sunday Express, 20 June 1982

The idea behind the scheme was for people to financially support the care of animals at the zoo but somehow Ernie managed to actually "adopt" the animal.

"The zoo lady said they pong a little at first, but after you get to know them they are really quite apppealing."

Daily Express, 5 May 1983

"We don't mind Grandma sharing our bedroom while we've got guests, but her embrocation and Evergreen ointment are the aggravation."

Daily Express, 29 December 1983

Even Mickey Mouse is disillusioned.

"Well that should put paid to the legend of Father Christmas."

Daily Express, 24 December 1984

"Oh Lord! I forgot – it's Mother's Day."

Sunday Express, 17 March 1985

I am not sure if Ernie's obviously serious illness relates to the prospect of school tomorrow
or the uniform he will be obliged to wear.

"I only asked him to try his new uniform for school tomorrow and he suddenly remembered he's got a recurrence of
an old dormant ailment."

Sunday Express, 5 January 1986

Giles, an avid sailor, usually introduced an appropriate cartoon on the day of the annual Boat Show at Earls Court. It seems here that the other members of the family, already geared to go, are keener on the trip than Father himself.

"Ahoy, there – I hope you haven't forgotten you're taking us all to the preview of the Boat Show today."

Daily Express, 5 January 1988

The Bathroom

The dog, as well as the children, looks guilty.

"Grandma can't find her Sunday dress – what was the Guy Fawkes you burnt on Friday wearing at the time?"

Sunday Express, 7 November 1954

The Russians had launched their Vostok 3 spacecraft three days earlier and would launch Vostok 4 the following day.
They orbited the Earth within sight of each other and it was the first time that more than one crewed spacecraft was
in orbit at the same time. In just short of three days, Vostok 4 completed 48 orbits of the Earth.

"The Russians have been round the world twice since Grandma's been in there."

Daily Express, 14 August 1962

I am not sure that he doesn't also have snakes in his bathroom.

"Those tenants who've only got snakes in their bathroom are lucky."

Sunday Express, 14 March 1965

The day before, the House of Commons had voted 356 to 244 in favour of joining the Common Market after decades of discussion.

"So much for Grandma's hunger strike if they voted us in the Common Market last night – that's the third haddock Vera's taken her up this morning."

Daily Express, 29 October 1971

The Stairs and Landing

Giles, a great sports car enthusiast with his own Jaguar XK120, took part in that year's *Daily Express* National Motor Rally. Father might, in fact, be pleased that the children are obviously inspired by his great passion.

"Daddy won't love little boys who play motors outside his bedroom the morning after four days' driving in the rally."

Sunday Express, 16 November 1952

The children were hoping to see the fight between Cassius Clay (Muhammed Ali) and Sonny Liston for the World Heavyweight Boxing Championship, being held that night in Miami Beach, Florida. Clay, at the time considered the underdog, won when Liston gave up at the opening of the seventh round after being dominated in the sixth. Father and Grandma are obviously preparing for the fight.

"Prize fights from Telstar at six in the morning is early enough – all transistor radios, if you please."

Daily Express, 25 February 1964

At this time, there were serious problems resulting from a combination of significant increases in oil prices from the Middle East and reduced coal stocks at home. Power cuts were a feature of everyday life and people became used to living under candlelight in the evenings.

"OK Grandma, I've found the little top ones you dropped – Butch has got 'em in his basket."

Daily Express, 17 January 1974

The price of tea had risen dramatically the day before this cartoon appeared and the government had announced that, under the 1974 Prices Act, it would force companies to reduce the price of tea by about 20 per cent. I do not think that any of the children will agree to Father's request, particularly Ernie.

"How would you like to be a brave boy and tell Grandma there's no more morning tea till the price comes down?"

Sunday Express, 26 February 1978

130 The new newspaper was published in Manchester and circulated only in the North and the Midlands. It was produced by Express Newspapers, to compete with the *Daily Mirror* and the *Sun* and was also intended to utilise the company's under-used presses in Manchester.

"Grandma! That's enough Ooh! Cor! Wow! and Well I never! We'd ALL like to have a look at the new *Daily Star*."

Daily Express, 2 November 1978

With a household already containing a range of animals, I am not sure that Father will completely welcome this level of commitment to the worthy concept of protecting our wildlife.

"Did you see the Wildfowl Trust suggest we all 'adopt a duck' to preserve the species. Can you imagine?"

Daily Express, 26 July 1979

As Giles's note indicates, Black Rod had been refused entrance into the House of Commons, an extremely rare event. The children have decided to treat Grandma in a similarly rude way.

"Children! Grandma's had enough 'You Michael Foot, she Black Rod' – open the door!"

Sunday Express, 16 November 1980

"Who's going to volunteer to tell Grandma that the delivery strike's been called off but Butch has eaten her Bingo page?"

Sunday Express, 3 January 1982

134 The Chancellor of the Exchequer, Sir Geoffrey Howe, presented his Budget that afternoon and one authority considered that it was "short on any new strategic thought". Obviously he had not considered Father's wish.

"Lord, whatever he taxes, please let him tax all transistor radios out of existence."

Daily Express, 9 March 1982

Luckily the advice was undermined by Grandma's addiction to the horses.

135

"It's all very well psychiatrists advising lock 'em in the loo when they're naughty – they don't have a grandma in there reading the racing page."

Daily Express, 19 October 1982

The day before, the *Daily Express* had run a competition to "win a racehorse". Although Grandma has always been a keen follower of the horses, this may be one animal too many in the Giles household.

"Mum, Grandma's won a *Daily Express* racehorse."

Daily Express, 25 October 1983

The twins appear to be enjoying the spectacle and George Jr. seems pleased with Mickey Mouse's antics.

137

"He does that every time British Rail put their fares up."

Sunday Express, 24 November 1985

The next day, about 117,000 BT engineers, unhappy with pay and working conditions, started a nationwide strike. It caused widespread difficulties for the country's business community as well as for private citizens. After two weeks of negotiations the strike finally ended on 11 February, following an agreed pay increase.

"You bet I'm shouting! Everyone's making as many calls as they can before the BT strike begins!"

Here Giles may have been referring to an attempt by Prime Minister Margaret Thatcher to introduce photo ID cards for travelling football fans that summer in an attempt to combat hooliganism.

"If we're all going to have Identity Cards, Grandma can use the same one she had in 1939."

Daily Express, 27 September 1988

As illustrated by Father's newspaper, the *Sunday Express* was promoting a healthy lifestyle but, as pointed out by his sister Bridget, Ernie was in danger of serious injury.

"It'll be extremely bad for your health if she hears you say 'Morning Fatso'."

Sunday Express, 8 January 1989

The Garden

Although this assault occurred during National Baby Week, which was first established in 1917, I am not sure that Father's first thoughts were strongly focused upon the general wellbeing of children.

"That's a nice thing to call baby on the first day of National Baby Week."

Sunday Express, 13 June 1954

142   The Associated Society of Locomotive Engineers and Firemen had called a strike on 28 May, which continued until 14 June. The situation became so intense that the government declared a State of Emergency on 31 May. Obviously Father's annoyance covered all aspects of rail travel.

"You ought to be ashamed – kicking their little trains all over the place just because you had to walk home."

Sunday Express, 5 June 1955

Three days earlier, Parliament had discussed the serious health dangers linked to smoking tobacco.

143

"Of course, you realise that if my Dad gives it up we shall have to start buying our own."

Sunday Express, 30 June 1957

In Giles's cartoon world, there was always a degree of rivalry between Grandma and Ernie but this seems a bit extreme – even his sister Bridget seems taken aback.

"There'll be some hollering when we get in – I locked Grandma in the bathroom before we went away."

Sunday Express, 11 August 1957

Three days earlier the USSR had put its satellite, Sputnik 3, into orbit with a dog, Laika, aboard. This caused some concern in the UK as it was known that the dog would not survive the experience. The children, led by neighbour Stinker, are providing additional evidence for, I suspect, Grandma's unhappiness regarding the use of an animal for such a purpose.

"Grandma says every time the new Russian Sputnik goes past she can hear a whole pack of dogs barking."

Sunday Express, 18 May 1958

146 This was a time when three major nations were experimenting with atom bombs. The UK was exploding a series of nuclear weapons on Christmas Island in the Pacific. About seven weeks after this cartoon appeared, US President Dwight Eisenhower announced a one-year moratorium on nuclear testing, effective from 31 October 1958, providing the Soviet Union and the UK also agreed to suspend testing. Britain had already indicated that it would do so, and the Soviet Union agreed on 30 August.

"Grandma says we'll all look silly sitting on a cloud playing harps with our heads off telling one another that the threat to drop the atom bomb was a hoax."

Daily Express, 6 July 1958

"Grandma! For heaven's sake forget there's a grandma competing in the Olympic Games – you're too late for the selectors, anyway."

This was National Census day. For the first time since the census was started in 1801, questions were asked about qualifications, migration status and household. Obviously Father's answers on the form regarding Grandma caused amazement among the children.

"What did he put in that damn Census Form that makes them go 'Cor!' every time they come to a bit about me?"

Sunday Express, 23 April 1961

There was national concern about an unbalanced flow of scientists and engineers to the USA from the UK, referred to as the "Brain Drain".

"If the Americans are over here buying all our scientific talent how come they missed you?"

Sunday Express, 3 March 1963

150 Elder Statesman and war leader Sir Winston Churchill announced his retirement from politics at this time but he remained an MP until the following year's general election on 15 October. Four weeks before this cartoon appeared, he became the first foreign national to receive honorary United States citizenship.

"Bet he doesn't wear it."

The trial of society osteopath Dr. Stephen Ward was being held at the Old Bailey with two glamorous star witnesses – 21-year-old showgirl Christine Keeler and Mandy Rice-Davies. The trial drew huge crowds outside the Court. The situation around the trial involved a sex scandal with a government minister and a Russian naval attache. No doubt, Grandma decided that a visit to the trial would further the children's education more than a visit to the Tower of London. Well, she would – wouldn't she?

"Grandma didn't take us to the Tower of London – she took us to the Old Bailey."

Sunday Express, 28 July 1963

152 Sir Francis Chichester was undertaking his epic single-handed voyage around the world, having left Plymouth on his 53-foot ketch, Gipsy Moth IV, on 27 August 1966. He arrived home on 28 May. He was knighted seven weeks before this cartoon appeared for his record of achievement in the navigation and handling of small craft.

"Every year I hope he'll forget it, but every year someone like Sir Francis Chichester makes the headlines."

Sunday Express, 19 March 1967

Of the 38 horses that started the 1971 Grand National, only 13 finished. Maybe Father's tip was good, but did not finish or was badly hampered.

"I don't think Mr Jones thought much of that tip Dad gave him for the National."

Sunday Express, 4 April 1971

Father and Grandma are of one mind on this occasion: horse racing at Epsom.

"That's right – you DID hear me tell them to go and get lost for four days up a mountain."

Sunday Express, 26 April 1973

The newspapers had reported that in the evening of 19 September, a fallen socket wrench punctured the fuel tank of a Titan missile loaded with a nuclear warhead at a US Air Force base near Arkansas. The fuel leak triggered a major explosion. Grandma does appear to be vulnerable.

"If that spanner lands on Grandma's nut you'll get more than a nuclear explosion."

Sunday Express, 21 September 1980

This was two days after the London Marathon and it is not recorded how Father fared.

"Like last year, Butch, forget walkies for a few days after his marathon."

The Vernal Equinox, when the sun crosses the equator, is around 20 March in the northern hemisphere and can, as illustrated here, herald the start of work in the garden after the winter period. For Father and Butch the dog it obviously means something different from Mother's understanding.

"When I said it's time we got the garden things out for Spring I was thinking more in the line of these."

Sunday Express, 20 March 1988

As shown in Grandma's newspaper, the country was suffering a spate of strikes and people began resorting to a range of alternative transport. Obviously Father's possible solution will not be pursued.

"Well, that's skateboards out as an alternative means of getting him to work."

Sunday Express, 14 May 1989

This could lead to interesting conversations between Mother and Father.

159

"Like me to fill it in for you?"

All the cartoons in this book were copied from material in Carl Giles's own private archive, a huge collection of artwork, ephemera and correspondence, which is held by the British Cartoon Archive at the University of Kent. Carl Giles had been cartoonist for Lord Beaverbrook's *Daily* and *Sunday Express* for almost 20 years, when on 20 March 1962 the Conservative M.P. Sir Martin Lindsay tabled a motion deploring "the conduct of Lord Beaverbrook in authorizing over the last few years in the newspapers controlled by him more than 70 adverse comments on members of the royal family who have no means of replying".

Lindsay was wrong about the royal family having no means of reply. That day Prince Philip also vented his anger at Beaverbrook's campaign, during a press reception at the British Embassy in Rio de Janeiro. According to the paper's Brazil representative, the Prince declared that, "The *Daily Express* is a bloody awful newspaper. It is full of lies, scandal and imagination. It is a vicious paper."

When the *Daily Express* reported this the next day, Giles decided to treat it as a joke. He knew the royal family enjoyed his cartoons; they often asked for the artwork. This had begun in 1948, when Prince Philip was sent a cartoon on the State Opening of Parliament, and over the next few years Giles received a steady stream of requests from Buckingham Palace for original drawings.

Left: *Lord Beaverbrook is marched to the Tower, 22 March 1962.*

Giles drew the diminutive Lord Beaverbrook being escorted through the Traitor's Gate at the Tower of London, with a headsman's axe and block standing ready in the background. The caption repeated Prince Philip's condemnation of the *Daily Express*, but added laconically: "'Ah well,' said Lord B., as they trotted him off to the Tower, 'at least he takes it or he wouldn't know it was a bloody awful newspaper.'"

This was a brilliant response, which did much to defuse the situation. When Giles's cartoon was printed the next day, *Daily Express* staff were surprised to receive a phone call from the Queen's press secretary, with a message for Giles that "Her Majesty requests today's cartoon to commemorate one of her husband's most glorious indiscretions."

Giles sent off the artwork and in May 1962 found himself invited to "a small informal luncheon party" at Buckingham Palace with the Queen and Prince Philip. "I was filled with absolute dread," Giles recalled afterwards. "But as soon as she started to talk I was put at my ease…There were about half a dozen corgis running about in a completely uncontrolled state. Suddenly the Queen shouted, 'HEP'. It was like a bark from a sergeant major. The corgis immediately stood to attention. Then filed out of the room."

After the lunch Giles mischievously drew a cartoon of the guests leaving with corgi-savaged trousers. He sent it to the Queen, who returned her thanks through one of her private secretaries, noting that she was "glad that you got away without having lost, at least to the best of her knowledge, so much as a shred of your trousers".

After that Giles became what one *Daily Express* journalist called "a kind of cartooning jester to the royal family". By the time he retired in 1991 the royal family had more than 40 of his original drawings, the largest number being owned by Prince Philip, who shared Giles's anarchic view of the world.

The British Cartoon Archive, based at the University of Kent's Templeman Library in Canterbury, is dedicated to the history of British cartooning over the last two hundred years. It holds the artwork for more than 150,000 British political and social-comment cartoons, plus large collections of comic strips, newspaper cuttings, books and magazines. Its website at www.cartoons.ac.uk has over 200,000 cartoon images, including the majority of Carl Giles's published work.